TABLE OF CONTENTS

For the Teacher

This reproducible study guide consists of lessons to use in conjunction with
A Single Shard. Written in chapter-by-chapter format, the guide contains a synopsis,
pre-reading activities, vocabulary and comprehension exercises, as well as extension
activities to be used as follow-up to the novel.

In a homogeneous classroom, whole class instruction with one title is
appropriate. In a heterogeneous classroom, reading groups should be formed: each
group works on a different novel at its reading level. Depending upon the length of time
devoted to reading in the classroom, each novel, with its guide and accompanying lessons, may be completed in three to six weeks.

Begin using NOVEL-TIES for guided reading by distributing the novel and
a folder to each child. Distribute duplicated pages of the study guide for students to
place in their folders. After examining the cover and glancing through the book,
students can participate in several pre-reading activities. Vocabulary questions
should be considered prior to reading a chapter or group of chapters; all other work
should be done after the chapter has been read. Comprehension questions can be
answered orally or in writing. The classroom teacher should determine the amount of
work to be assigned, always keeping in mind that readers must be nurtured and that
the ultimate goal is encouraging students' love of reading.

The benefits of using NOVEL-TIES are numerous. Students read good
literature in the original, rather than in abridged or edited form. The good reading
habits will be transferred to the books students read independently. Passive readers
become active, avid readers.

SYNOPSIS

This story is set in Ch'ulp'o, a potter's village in twelfth-century Korea. An elderly man called Crane-man, because he has one shriveled leg, is raising Tree-ear, an orphan named for a mushroom that grows "without benefit of parent seed." Crane-man and Tree-ear, now twelve, make their home under a bridge.

Tree-ear admires the work of Min, the most skillful of all the town's craftsmen, but accidentally breaks a piece of his work. When Tree-ear offers to pay his debt in servitude, Min grudgingly agrees. Anticipating that Min will teach him how to make beautiful celadon pottery, he is disappointed to be given the laborious task of chopping wood for the kiln. Once his period of servitude ends, Tree-ear offers to work without pay. Min accepts Tree-ear's services, but never shows him how to make a pot.

Although not taught the craft of pottery, Tree-ear benefits from the generosity of Min's wife. She provides him with extra food and spare clothing for Crane-man. From the other potters, Tree-ear learns that Min is a perfectionist whose dream is to receive a royal commission. When the royal emissary Kim arrives in the village, Min sees an opportunity to fulfill this desire.

Kang, one of the other village potters, impresses Emissary Kim with a new inlay technique, but not by the imperfections in his pottery. The emissary is also impressed by Min's work. The potters who garnered special attention take the opportunity during a temporary absence of the emissary to work feverishly on one last piece that might determine which potter will receive the commission.

Telling Min about Kang's inlay work, Tree-ear motivates his master to incorporate this technique into his vases. When the vases are fired however, they are all suffused with a brown tint, causing Min to smash them. When the emissary returns, Min is unable to show him any new work, and a limited commission goes to Kang. Tree-ear is distressed that Min does not show the emissary the shards from his vases, which would indicate the value of his work. Although Emissary Kim agrees to see any new work that Min creates, Min cannot travel to Songdo, the capital. To repay the kindness of Min's wife, Tree-ear offers to make the trip. She agrees on the condition that he return safely and call her by the endearing name *Ajima* or "Auntie."

Tree-ear finally gains the courage to ask Min to teach him the skill of making a vase on the potter's wheel. Min angrily refuses because it is traditional for the potter's trade to be passed on from father to son. Disheartened, Tree-ear goes about his work with little joy. He finds some consolation, however, in molding small clay figures by hand.

After Min makes the new vases, Crane-man creates a straw container to hold them during Tree-ear's journey to Songdo. Ajima agrees to feed Crane-man during the boy's absence in return for doing chores. Before he leaves, the boy gives Crane-man a little monkey figure that he has made, which the old man proudly attaches to his waist.

Tree-ear travels safely until he reaches the city of Puyo, where Crane-man has requested he visit the Rock of the Falling Flowers. It was there that the female attendants of the king of Paekche showed great courage by leaping from the cliff, like falling flowers, rather than be taken prisoner by the T'ang Chinese. While at the site, Tree-ear is beset by robbers, who take his money and throw the vases off the cliff. Distraught, Tree-ear runs down in hopes that one of the vases will be saved. Sadly, there remains only a single shard large enough to display the inlay work and the fine technique of his master. Tree-ear resolutely continues on to Songdo with this shard and shows it to Emissary Kim, who recognizes the excellent work and awards Min a commission.

Once home, Tree-ear rushes to tell the potter about the commission. Min and Ajima's pleasure is tempered by sad news: Crane-man has died. After mourning the loss of his friend, Tree-ear arrives for work as usual the next morning. Min orders him to cut large logs for a new potter's wheel, one for Tree-ear to use. Min will at last teach the boy how to make celadon pottery. To add to Tree-ear's joy, Ajima tells him that he is to live with them and take the name *Hyung-pil*, which contains a syllable from the name of her dead son—an honor bestowed on siblings. Tree-ear is an orphan no more.

BACKGROUND INFORMATION

Koryo Period

In its ancient history, the land we now know as Korea was divided into kingdoms. As one kingdom would gain power, it would unify the land under its domain. The kingdoms were unified under the northern state of Koryo from A.D. 918 to 1392. The name "Koryo" derives from "Koguryo" and is the root of the modern name "Korea."

The Koryo period was beset by internal problems and wars with China, Manchuria, and Japan. This same period, however, was marked by many achievements. In this period of peace following a treaty with China in 1022, there was a blossoming of culture that led to great advances in scholarship and art. One of the crowning achievements of the period was a distinctive ceramics industry, which developed the unique gray-green celadon stoneware now hailed as one of Korea's greatest contributions to the fine arts.

Celadon Pottery

Celadon is a type of ceramic pottery that exhibits both beauty and grace, demonstrating a unique combination of classical form and artistic expression. Korean potters borrowed techniques from those of the Sung Dynasty in China. Plain celadon reflected the traditional technique and style imported from Sung China. It was, however, distinguished by its elegance and its unique color, achieved with a bluish-green glaze.

Pottery is a result of clay, fire, and glaze. Korean celadon begins with white clay, which is purified and then shaped on the potter's wheel. The vessels are then engraved with designs, covered with glaze, and baked in a kiln at a high temperature.

Korean potters improved on their work by developing an inlay technique around the twelfth century. They made pattern incisions in the vessels and then filled them in with a white or black slip, a semi-liquid form of clay. Next, the vessels would be fired in a kiln. After this, they would be covered with a celadon glaze and then fired once more.

Buddhism

Buddhism, a religion popular in the early part of the Koryo dynasty, originated in India and came to Korea first through China. Buddhism teaches that the goal of the faithful is to achieve nirvana, a blissful state of insight and release from the bonds of self and the world. The state of spiritual perfection is achieved through the practice of humility, generosity, mercy, restraint from violence, and self-control.

During the Koryo dynasty, the state supported Buddhist temples. The monks were not taxed and were influential in the king's court. Buddhism became an economic power as well as a spiritual influence in Koryo. It also brought the community together at ritual observances in the temples, providing a means of release of daily stress through prayer, and stimulating scholarship and study. The monks also served the community by caring for the unfortunate, such as orphans and the homeless, by taking them into the temples.

MAP OF 12TH CENTURY KOREA

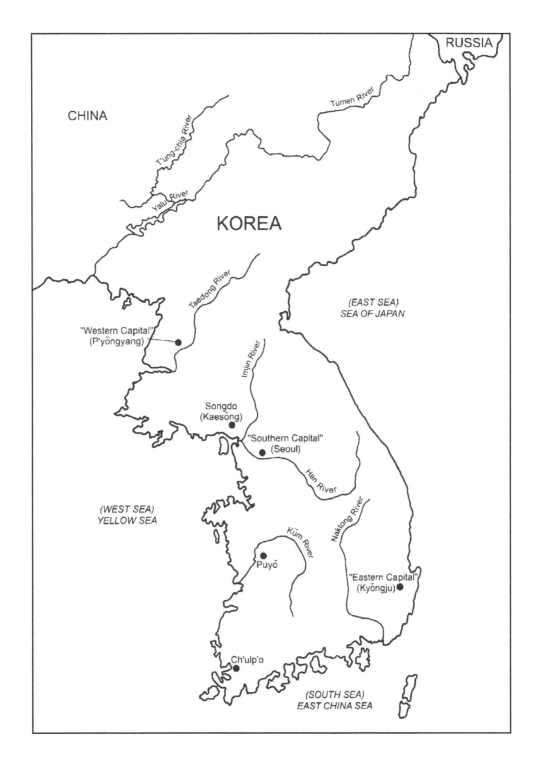

PRE-READING ACTIVITIES

1. Preview the book by reading the title and the author's name and by looking at the illustration on the cover. A *shard* is a piece of broken earthenware or pottery. Knowing this, what do you think the story will be about? Where and when do you think it takes place? Have you read any other books by the same author?

2. Read the Background Information on page three of this study guide and do some additional research on twelfth-century Korea. Then fill in the first two columns of a K-W-L chart, such as the one below. When you finish the book, return to the chart to complete the third column.

Twelfth-Century Korea

What I Know −K−	What I Want to Learn −W−	What I Learned −L−

3. Have you read any other books of fiction or seen any films that take place in Korea in the present or in the past? If so, what did you learn about life at that time?

4. If possible, obtain a film or find a book that shows a potter working at a potter's wheel. Follow the steps of this exacting process to have a better appreciation of this craft. Also, try to find color photographs or actual examples of celadon-glazed pottery. Display this in the classroom while you are reading.

5. With your classmates, discuss how young people today determine their futures and the work they will do. As you read the book, compare these criteria with those that faced Tree-ear, the main character.

6. *A Single Shard* is a book of historical fiction—one that uses history as a background for imagined events. The characters in such a work may be fictional or historical or both. What other works of historical fiction have you read? What do you enjoy about this type of book? What information does it give you that you would not be able to get by reading a history book?

7. *A Single Shard* won the Newberry Medal in 2002. Read about John Newberry's life and about the Newberry award. Why is the medal awarded? What other Newberry Award books have you read?

8. Look at the map of ancient Korea on page four of this study guide. As you read the book, trace the journey Tree-ear makes from Ch'ulp'o to Songdo (Kaesong).

9. The author uses chapter numbers instead of titles. As you finish each chapter, write a title that conveys the main idea.

Chapter	Chapter Title
Chapter 1	
Chapter 2	
Chapter 3	
Chapter 4	
Chapter 5	
Chapter 6	
Chapter 7	
Chapter 8	
Chapter 9	
Chapter 10	
Chapter 11	
Chapter 12	
Chapter 13	

CHAPTERS 1, 2

Vocabulary: Choose a word from the Word Box to replace each underlined word or phrase in the following sentences. Write the word on the line below the sentence.

WORD BOX				
arid	cowered	impudence	oblivious	precariously
complied	derision	momentum	perusal	prosperity

1. After a <u>careful reading</u> of the movie titles, Roy finally found the video he wanted.

   _____

2. The book was so interesting that I was <u>not mindful</u> to my surroundings.

   _____

3. Desert lands are <u>dry</u>.

   _____

4. Everyone appreciates a time of peace and <u>good fortune</u>.

   _____

5. When the doctor ordered my mother to get some bed rest, she readily <u>obeyed</u>.

   _____

6. A falling object gains <u>force of movement</u> as it falls.

   _____

7. The dog <u>crouched in fear</u> under the table after being scolded.

   _____

8. After talking back to his teacher, she scolded him for his <u>shameless boldness</u>.

   _____

9. The hikers walked <u>dangerously</u> close to the edge of the cliff.

   _____

10. His strange way of dressing leaves him open to the <u>scornful laughter</u> of his classmates.

   _____

Chapters 1, 2 (cont.)

Read to find out why Tree-ear starts to work for Min.

Questions:

1. Why do Tree-ear and Crane-man greet each other by saying, "Have you *hungered* well today?"

2. How is Tree-ear's behavior rewarded by the farmer?

3. What is the relationship between Tree-ear and Crane-man?

4. Why does Tree-ear like to watch Min at work?

5. Why isn't Min secretive about his work as are the other potters in the village?

6. Why does Min think that Tree-ear is a thief? What changes his mind?

7. Why does Tree-ear offer to work for the potter to pay for the broken container?

8. In what way is Tree-ear's first day working for Min a disappointment?

9. How does Crane-man help Tree-ear when he returns home from his first day working for Min?

Questions for Discussion:

1. Do you think Tree-ear acted in a decent manner when he waited before alerting the farmer of the hole in his sack?

2. What does Crane-man mean when he tells Tree-ear that, "Scholars read the great works of the world. But you and I must learn to read the world itself"?

3. Do you think Min treats Tree-ear fairly? Is it possible to judge Min by today's standards?

4. If you were Tree-ear, would you go back to work for Min?

5. Do you think that Crane-man is a proper guardian for a boy? What does Tree-ear gain by living with Crane-man? What does he lack?

Chapters 1, 2 (cont.)

Literary Device: Metaphor

A metaphor is a suggested or implied comparison. For example:

> As he [Tree-ear] heaved a large, rough log, an arrow of pain shot through his right hand.

What is being compared?

_____

Why is this better than saying, "Tree-ear's hand hurt"?

_____

_____

Literary Element: Setting

In literature, the setting refers to the time and place in which the story occurs.

What is the setting of this novel?

_____

What details about the setting make the characters' time and lifestyle seem real?

_____

_____

_____

Writing Activity:

Imagine that you are Min. Write a journal entry for the day that you met Tree-ear. Record your thoughts and feelings about the boy, and tell why you decided to let him work for you.

CHAPTERS 3, 4

Vocabulary: Draw a line from each word on the left to its definition on the right. Then use the numbered words to fill in the blanks in the sentences below.

1. ministrations		a.	abrupt
2. diligent		b.	that which remains after a part is removed
3. insolence		c.	playful teasing
4. curt		d.	hard-working
5. felicitous		e.	be enough
6. residue		f.	services
7. suffice		g.	highly respected elderly man
8. crucial		h.	appropriate
9. patriarch		i.	bold rudeness
10. banter		j.	very important

. . . .

1. The impatient clerk gave the customer a(n) _____ reply.

2. This is the _____ game that will decide the championship.

3. Eggs and bacon is a(n) _____ combination for breakfast.

4. Once my grandfather dies, my father, being the oldest son, will become the family _____.

5. The patient recovered sooner than expected because of the _____ of her attentive nurse.

6. The _____ student kept on working until he had finished his report.

7. There was much good-natured _____ among friends going on at the party.

8. After you have eaten a large breakfast, a light lunch will _____.

9. Ashamed of her son's _____, the mother required him to apologize to her guests.

10. The syrup on the unwashed plate dried up, leaving a sticky _____.

Chapters 3, 4 (cont.)

Read to learn about Min's dilemma.

Questions:

1. Why does Tree-ear continue to work for Min despite his scolding?
2. How does Min make Tree-ear extremely happy?
3. Why does Tree-ear adjust to the new task of digging clay more quickly than he did to chopping wood?
4. How does Min's wife make life more pleasant for Tree-ear?
5. Why does Tree-ear feel shame when he hears how Crane-man lost his crutch?
6. Why is the hidden bowl always full when Tree-ear comes to retrieve it?
7. What gives the celadon pottery its distinct color?
8. How does Tree-ear's lowly status help him obtain vital information?
9. What does Tree-ear learn about Min's work from the other potters?

Questions for Discussion:

1. Do you think that Tree-ear's resentment of Min is justified? Why do you suppose Min never hit him after the first time he mistook him for a thief?
2. Do you think that Min will ever teach Tree-ear how to make a pot? Why does he give Tree-ear so few verbal instructions at each new step in preparing clay for pottery?
3. How does the way the homeless were treated in Tree-ear's time and place compare with the way they are treated today in your community?

Literary Devices:

I. *Personification*—Personification is a literary device in which an author grants human qualities to nonhuman objects. For example:

> The clay made squelching, sucking noises, as if it were trying to swallow the spade.

What is being personified?

_____

What does this suggest about the job of digging clay?

_____

_____

Chapters 3, 4 (cont.)

II. *Simile*—A simile is a figure of speech in which a comparison between two unlike objects is stated directly using the words "like" or "as." For example:

> Tree-ear's joy at being forgiven was like a wisp of smoke; Min's orders for the day blew it into nothingness.

What is being compared?

_____

What does this reveal about Tree-ear's feelings?

_____

_____

Find another simile in these two chapters and write it on the lines below. Then tell what is being compared.

_____

_____

_____

Writing Activities:

1. Write about a time when you were scolded unjustly. How did you react to the scolding? How was everything resolved?

2. Imagine you are Tree-ear. Write a thank-you note to Min's wife to thank her for her kindness.

Chapters 3, 4 (cont.)

Literary Element: Characterization

The reader learns about characters by what they do, say, and think, and by what others say about them. In the chart below, list important information you have learned about the major story characters. Continue to add information to the chart as you read the book.

Character	Physical Appearance	Personality Traits
Tree-ear		
Crane-man		
Min		
Min's wife		

CHAPTERS 5, 6

Vocabulary: Use the words in the Word Box and the clues below to complete the crossword puzzle.

WORD BOX				
arduous	entourage	feign	lugubrious	tithe
connoisseur	envision	impassive	pretense	translucent
emissary	explicit	invective	surreptitiously	

Across

4. too sad; overly mournful
5. pretend
7. false appearance
9. group of attendants
11. without feeling or emotion
15. letting light through without being transparent
16. picture in one's mind

Down

1. stealthily; secretly
2. tax for the support of the church
3. critical judge of art or matters of taste
6. violent attack in words
8. person sent on a mission or errand
10. hard to do; using up much energy
12. clearly expressed

Chapters 5, 6 (cont.)

> Read to learn about Min's dilemma.

Questions:

1. How do Kang's actions arouse Tree-ear's suspicions?

2. What does Tree-ear find puzzling when he examines spillage from two small bowls that Kang was carrying?

3. Why does Tree-ear worry about the approach of winter?

4. How does Crane-man acquire a warm winter jacket?

5. What is Kang's secret? Why doesn't Tree-ear reveal this secret to Min?

6. How does the news of the emissary's impending visit affect the village?

7. Why does Tree-ear think that Kang might receive a royal commission?

8. What gives Min some hope that he might get a commission?

Questions for Discussion:

1. Do you think that Tree-ear should have told Min about Kang's pottery?

2. How do you think the death of Min's son has affected him? Do you think it has anything to do with the way he treats Tree-ear?

3. In what ways might Min have already begun teaching Tree-ear to become a potter?

Literary Devices:

I. *Metaphor*—What is being compared in the following metaphor?

> The flame of hope that burned in him [Tree-ear] was smaller now, but no less bright or fierce, and he tended it almost daily with visions of the pot he would make.

_____

What does this reveal about Tree-ear?

_____

_____

_____

Chapters 5, 6 (cont.)

II. *Personification*—What is being personified in the following passage?

> Soon winter rode on the back of the wind as it swept down the
> mountain slopes toward the village.

_____

What does this reveal about the climate?

_____

_____

Literary Element: Conflict

A *conflict* is a struggle between opposing forces. An *external conflict* is a character's struggle against an outside force, such as nature, fate, or another person. An *internal conflict* is a personal struggle that takes place within a character's mind. In a chart such as the one below, indicate the conflicts you have come upon in this story so far. Indicate the possible resolution of each conflict. After you finish the story, tell how each conflict was actually resolved.

Conflicts	Possible Resolutions	Actual Resolutions
Internal Conflicts		
External Conflicts		

Writing Activity:

Imagine that you are the emissary. Write a report giving your suggestions about who should receive a royal commission.

CHAPTERS 7, 8

Vocabulary: Antonyms are words with opposite meanings. Draw a line from each word in column A to its antonym in column B. Then use the words in column A to fill in the blanks in the sentences below.

A	B
1. haranguing	a. happy
2. exulted	b. praising
3. plaintive	c. attentive
4. intricate	d. calmly
5. noxious	e. excitement
6. remiss	f. simple
7. serenity	g. grieved
8. frenetically	h. healthful

. . . .

1. That _____ song always brings tears to my eyes.

2. I closed the windows to block out _____ automobile fumes.

3. The fans _____ over the victory of their favorite team.

4. Since she waited until the last minute to work on her report, she worked _____ to finish it on time.

5. As a babysitter, I would be _____ if I did not keep an eye on the children as they played in their rooms.

6. It is better to provide an example of good behavior instead of _____ a child for every mistake.

7. I achieved a feeling of _____ as I did nothing but watch the waves roll gently onto the shore.

8. The instructions for building the model plane were too _____ for a beginner to follow.

Chapters 7, 8 (cont.)

> Read to find out whether Min will show Tree-ear how to make a pot.

Questions:

1. Why does Min send Tree-ear for white and red clay?

2. What does Tree-ear realize as he drains the clay for Min?

3. How does Min's work pattern and mood change as he awaits the emissary's return?

4. Why does Min smash his own vases?

5. Why does Tree-ear offer to journey to Songdo with Min's pottery?

6. Under what conditions will Min's wife allow Tree-ear to go to Songdo? What does this suggest about her feelings for the boy?

7. Why does Tree-ear fear the journey to Songdo? How does Crane-man allay his fears?

8. What is Min's reaction when Tree-ear asks the potter to teach him how to make a pot?

Questions for Discussion:

1. Which do you think is a better way to instruct—by example and practice or by verbal instruction?

2. Do you think it is necessary for a potter to acquire the basic skills of preparing the kiln and clay before learning how to throw a pot on the wheel?

3. Why do you think Min reacts so strongly to Tree-ear's request to learn how to make a pot? What, if anything, do you think the boy can do to get him to change his mind?

4. Predict how Min's harsh words will affect Tree-ear. Do you think he will still make the journey to Songdo? Will he continue to work for Min?

Writing Activity:

Tree-ear fears going on the long journey to Songdo. Write about a time when you feared tackling a major task that you had never tried before. Could Crane-man's advice to Tree-ear have helped you? How?

CHAPTERS 9, 10

Vocabulary: Analogies are equations in which the first pair of words has the same relationship as the second pair of words. For example: RAPID is to SLOW as HEAVY is to LIGHT. Both pairs of words are opposites. Choose the best word from the Word Box to complete each of the analogies.

WORD BOX			
decreed	foraging	impeccable	progressively
endeavor	grimacing	meager	trepidation

1. FORCEFULLY is to POWERFULLY as INCREASINGLY is to _____.

2. CAUTIOUS is to RECKLESS as _____ is to FLAWED.

3. SCOWLING is to _____ as SLEEPING is to DOZING.

4. _____ is to EFFORT as FOE is to ENEMY.

5. RESPECT is to SCORN as CONFIDENCE is to _____.

6. GENEROUS is to _____ as SAD is to JOYOUS.

7. _____ is to ORDERED as HESITATED is to PAUSED.

8. RESEARCHING is to FACTS as _____ is to FOOD.

Read to find out how Tree-ear progresses on his journey.

Questions:

1. Why wouldn't Tree-ear find another master even if he left Ch'ulp'o?

2. How does a "second door blow open" for Tree-ear?

3. How do both Ajima and Tree-ear trick Crane-man into eating his meals at Min's house during Tree-ear's journey? Why does Crane-man accept the offer?

4. How does Crane-man react to Tree-ear's gift of the monkey?

5. Why is Tree-ear startled when Min touches him on the shoulder before he leaves on his journey?

6. In what ways is Tree-ear's journey easier than he expected?

7. How is Tree-ear's encounter with a fox like the one Crane-man experienced?

8. Why does Crane-man want Tree-ear to visit the Rock of the Falling Flowers?

9. Why does it become urgent for Tree-ear to get Min's work to Songdo?

Chapters 9, 10 (cont.)

Questions for Discussion:

1. In what ways have both Crane-man and Min been hampered by pride? Do you know of any such cases in your own experience?

2. Do you think Crane-man's story about his encounter with a fox helped or hindered Tree-ear when he met his fox?

3. Discuss the different ways there are to show true courage.

Literary Devices

I. *Metaphor*—What is being compared in the following metaphor?

> He [Tree-ear] moved on, swept along by the river of traffic.

_____

Why is this a good comparison?

_____

_____

II. *Building Suspense*—How does the author build suspense in the moments prior to Tree-ear's encounter with the fox?

_____

_____

Social Studies Connection:

The story of the T'ang invasion takes place during the time of the Three Kingdoms—Koguryŏ, Silla, and Paekche. Find out more about this era in Korean history and about the T'ang and Silla invasion of Paekche.

Writing Activity:

After his encounter with the fox, Tree-ear thinks, "We are afraid of the things we do not know—just because we do not know them." Write about a time when you or someone you know feared something due to ignorance.

CHAPTERS 11–13

Vocabulary: Synonyms are words with similar meanings. Draw a line from each word in column A to its synonym in column B. Then use the words in column A to fill in the blanks in the sentences below.

A		B	
1.	quell	a.	bound
2.	pallor	b.	unbelieving
3.	contorted	c.	paleness
4.	pinioned	d.	brightness
5.	jovial	e.	reserved
6.	incredulous	f.	twisted
7.	chastened	g.	confusion
8.	radiance	h.	punished
9.	subdued	i.	overcome
10.	welter	j.	merry

. . . .

1. The clown _____ his face until it looked so funny that all the children began to laugh.

2. My teacher appeared _____ when I told her my report was ruined in the washing machine.

3. The _____ of ideas coming from the members of the committee made it impossible for them to agree on a plan.

4. He was able to _____ his fear of flying by learning all he could about airplanes.

5. The _____ of the sun shines down on earth.

6. The bank robbers _____ the guard's arms.

7. While one of the twins was very talkative and lively, his brother was quite _____.

8. The _____ of her complexion was due to a long illness.

9. The little boy was _____ by his mother for his rude behavior.

10. She is in a(n) _____ mood because today is her birthday celebration.

Chapters 11–13 (cont.)

> Read to find out how Tree-ear's life changes after his return.

Questions:

1. Why are the robbers angry to find only vases in Tree-ear's *jiggeh*? Why do they break the vases?

2. Why does Tree-ear decide not to leap from the cliff after the robbery?

3. Why does Tree-ear believe that the single shard might impress the emissary?

4. How does Emissary Kim differ from his assistant?

5. How does Tree-ear feel when Emissary Kim awards Min a commission?

6. What surprises Tree-ear about Min's reaction when he tells the potter about the commission? What is the reason for this reaction?

7. How does Min's attitude toward Tree-ear change after the boy's return?

8. What surprising events occur the day after Tree-ear's return?

9. What is the significance of Ajima giving Tree-ear the name Hyung-pil?

Questions for Discussion:

1. In what different ways does Tree-ear show true courage? What other characters have you read about or seen in the movies who have displayed the same type of courage?

2. What legacy does Crane-man leave Tree-ear? How well do you think Min will fill Crane-man's shoes?

3. How do you think Ajima and Min's lives will be enriched by adopting Tree-ear?

4. Do you think the fictional account of Tree-ear represents a likely story about the maker of the "Thousand Cranes Vase"?

Literary Device: Simile

What is compared in the following simile?

> The day was chilly, autumn fully arrived, but her welcome swept over Tree-ear like a warm breeze.

_____

How does this help describe Tree-ear's feelings for Ajima?

_____

_____

Chapters 11–13 (cont.)

Literary Elements:

I. *Resolution*—In a novel the resolution is the part of the plot that presents the final outcome. The resolution shows how the major conflicts are resolved. Go back and look at the conflicts you listed on page sixteen of this guide. Tell how each one is resolved.

II. *Theme*—Theme refers to the author's message or the central idea in a literary work. In the chart below, record what the novel is saying about such topics as friendship, courage, determination, and responsibility. Add other topics to the chart.

Themes	Message
friendship	
courage	
determination	
responsibility	

Art Connection:

Reread the paragraph in italics at the end of the book. Make a drawing of the "Thousand Cranes Vase" or find a picture that shows a similar vase.

Writing Activity:

Imagine that you are a reporter writing about the potters who have received a royal commission. Write an article about Min and his apprentice, Hyung-pil. You should include quotations from the characters in your article.

CLOZE ACTIVITY

The following passage has been taken from Chapter Eleven of the novel. Read it through completely and then fill in each blank with a word that makes sense. Afterwards, you may compare your language with that of the author.

The second vase, its fall cushioned however slightly by the sand, had broken into bigger pieces. The largest shard was the size of his _____.[1] Tree-ear picked up this piece and swished _____[2] through the water to rinse off the _____.[3]

Across one side of the shard ran _____[4] shallow groove, evidence of the vase's melon _____.[5] Part of an inlaid peony blossom with _____[6] stem and leaves twined along the groove. _____[7] the glaze still shone clear and pure, _____[8] by the violence that had just been _____[9] it.

A sharp edge of the shard _____[10] into Tree-ear's palm. The pain was an _____[11]—he remembered now. It was when he _____[12] thrown the shard from the first batch _____[13] ruined vases into the river in Ch'ulp'o. _____[14] long ago it seemed!

Suddenly, Tree-ear raised _____[15] head. He stood up and squared his _____,[16] still clutching the piece of pottery. He _____[17] the shard carefully on a flat stone. _____[18] took the clay turtle from his waist _____[19] and squeezed it back into a ball. _____[20] he rolled the clay between his palms _____[21] it formed a long snake. Picking up _____[22] shard again, he pinched the snake all _____[23] way around the sharp edge to protect _____.[24]

Tree-ear removed the flint stones from his _____[25] pouch; they might scratch the shard. He _____[26] them into one corner of his tunic, _____[27] put the clay-bound shard into the pouch. _____[28] the pouch clear of the boulders with _____[29] hand, he climbed back to the path.

_____[30] every movement was quick with purpose; to _____[31] was to doubt. He had to make up his mind: he would journey on to Songdo and show the emissary the single shard.

POST-READING ACTIVITIES

1. Return to the K-W-L chart that you began in the Pre-Reading Activities. Correct any errors that you made in column one and fill in column three with information you learned while reading the book. Compare your findings with those of your classmates.

2. Return to the chapter title activity in the Pre-Reading Activities on page six of this study guide. Fill in chapte title you omitted. Compare your titles with those of your classmates while reviewing the sequence of events in the book.

3. Return to the characterization chart you began on page thirteen of this study guide. Add any further information you found.

4. Analyze one character from the novel by answering the following questions:

   • What did you like about this character?

   • What didn't you like about this character?

   • How are you and the character alike?

   • How are you and the character different?

   • Did this character change during the course of the story? If so, how?

5. Read the Author's Note at the end of the book. Why do you think the author included this information? How does it help you to better appreciate and understand the story? Would you have preferred to read this information before you read the novel?

6. **Oral Language Activity:** The scenes listed below never appeared in the book. With a small group of your classmates, role-play any of the following scenes by using your imagination to decide what the characters would have said. You may record your scene and play it for the entire class.

   • Tree-ear tells Min his feelings about the potter's refusal to teach him how to make a pot.

   • Ajima talks to Tree-ear about the loss of her son and its affect on Min.

   • Crane-man and Ajima talk about Tree-ear while he is on his journey to Songdo.

   • Ajima and Min talk about adopting Tree-ear after Crane-man's death.

   • Emissary Kim visits Min, Ajima, and Tree-ear to check on the progress of the vases for the palace.

7. Imagine that ten years have gone by. Write a brief sequel to the novel, telling what has happened to Tree-ear.

Post-Reading Activities (cont.)

8. Think of a friend who would enjoy reading *A Single Shard*. Write a letter recommending the novel to your friend. In your letter, briefly summarize the plot without revealing too much of the story. Try to include at least three reasons why you think your friend would enjoy this book.

9. **Social Studies / Art Connection:** With a group of your classmates, create a bulletin board collage that illustrates everyday life in Korea in the twelfth century. Include photocopied or original drawings of people's dress, a *jiggeh*, a potter's wheel, a kiln, a rice field, and other common sights. Write captions that tell about the pictures in the collage.

10. **Cooperative Learning Activity:** Work with a small group of your classmates to fill in a chart, such as the one below. Write the following adjectives beneath the names of the characters they might describe. You may use a word in more than one place and add words of your own.

aloof	grave	loyal	skillful
brave	intelligent	observant	stubborn
considerate	hard-working	polite	unjust
generous	honest	proud	warm-hearted

Tree-ear	Crane-man	Min	Ajima

SUGGESTIONS FOR FURTHER READING

Fiction

* Buck, Pearl S. *The Big Wave*. HarperCollins.

* Carlson, Natalie Savage. *The Family Under the Bridge*. HarperCollins.

Choi, Sook Nyui. *Echoes of the White Giraffe*. HMH Books.

* _____. *Year of Impossible Goodbyes*. Yearling.

Fox, Paula. *Monkey Island*. Yearling.

Fritsch, Debra M., and Ruth S. Hunter. *A Part of the Ribbon*. Turtle Press.

Holman, Sheri. *Sondok: Princess of the Moon and Stars*. Scholastic.

* Lai, Thanhha. *Inside Out and Back Again*. HarperCollins.

* McGraw, Eloise Jarvis. *The Golden Goblet*. Puffin.

Neuberger, Anne E. *The Girl-Son*. Carolrhoda Books.

Huynh, Quang Nhuong. *Water Buffalo Days*. HarperCollins.

Park, Frances and Ginger. *My Freedom Trip*. Boyds Mills Press.

* Paterson, Katherine. *The Master Puppeteer*. HarperTeen.

* _____. *The Sign of the Chrysanthemum*. Harper Trophy.

* Paulsen, Gary. *The Crossing*. Scholastic.

Riordan, James. *Korean Folk-tales*. Oxford University Press.

* Uchida, Yoshiko. *A Jar of Dreams*. Aladdin.

* Watkins, Yoko Kawashima. *So Far From the Bamboo Grove*. HarperCollins.

Nonfiction

Adams, Edward B. *Korea's Pottery Heritage*. Charles E. Tuttle.

Itoh, Ikutaro, and Yukata Mino. *The Radiance of Jade and the Clarity of Water: Korean Ceramics from the Ataka Collection, Osaka*. Hudson Hills Press.

Ries, Julien. *The Many Faces of Buddhism (Religions of Humanity)*. Chelsea House.

Other Books by Linda Sue Park

The Kite Fighters. HMH Books.

* *A Long Walk to Water*. HMH Books.

Seesaw Girl. HMH Books.

* *When My Name Was Keoko*. HMH Books.

*NOVEL-TIES Study Guides are available for these titles.

ANSWER KEY

Chapters 1, 2

Vocabulary: 1. perusal   2. oblivious   3. arid   4. prosperity   5. complied   6. momentum   7. cowered   8. impudence   9. precariously   10. derision

Questions: 1. Since Tree-ear and Crane-man are homeless and eat little, they use *hungered* instead of *eaten*, which is used in the usual greeting by well-fed villagers. 2. By alerting the farmer of the hole in his sack, Tree-ear is rewarded by being permitted to collect all that has sifted out. 3. Crane-man has cared for the orphaned Tree-ear since he was two-years-old and acts as a father toward the boy. 4. Tree-ear likes to watch Min at work because he admires his skill above all the other potters in the village and is fascinated by the care he takes in making his pottery, rejecting work that looks perfect to his uneducated eye. 5. Min is not secretive about his work because it is so far superior to the work of the other potters that he does not fear it can be replicated. 6. Min thinks that Tree-ear is a thief because he sees the boy at his house examining containers that he made. He changes his mind when Tree-ear repeats Crane-man's wisdom saying, "Stealing and begging make a man no better than a dog." 7. Tree-ear offers to work for Min because he is ashamed that he broke the container and owes the potter a debt. He also wants to know more about making pottery. 8. Tree-ear is disappointed on his first day at work because Min gives him the difficult task of chopping wood instead of teaching him how to make pottery as he had hoped. 9. Crane-man makes Tree-ear eat, acquires herbs to make a paste for the boy's wound, applies the paste, and bandages the wound.

Chapters 3, 4

Vocabulary: 1. f   2. d   3. i   4. a   5. h   6. b   7. e   8. j   9. g   10. c; 1. curt   2. crucial   3. felicitous   4. patriarch   5. ministrations   6. diligent   7. banter   8. suffice   9. insolence   10. residue

Questions: 1. Tree-ear continues to work for Min because he is willing to endure hardship in order to learn how to make pottery. 2. Min makes Tree-ear extremely happy when he grants the boy's wish to work for him even though he will not be paid for his labor. 3. Tree-ear is more quickly able to adjust to the task of collecting clay because the muscles in his back and arms have been strengthened by his days of woodcutting. 4. Min's wife makes life more pleasant for Tree-ear by giving him a nourishing meal and by being kind and pleasant toward him. She also refills his bowl so that Tree-ear can take food home for Crane-man. 5. Tree-ear is ashamed that he had a good lunch while Crane-man lost his crutch trying to obtain flounder. If Tree-ear had not been digging for clay, he would have exercised his usual agility to spear the fish that had come too close to shore. 6. Min's wife must be filling up the hidden bowl for Tree-ear because she realizes that he needs to bring food home to Crane-man. 7. A glaze made with wood ash gives the celadon pottery its distinct pale-green color. 8. Because of his lowly status, people ignore Tree-ear or speak as if he isn't there. In this way, he has been able to find out which rubbish heaps will lead to a better meal. 9. Tree-ear learns that Min works slowly and is a perfectionist, thus he needs to sell his pieces at a high price. He also learns that Min needs a royal commission in order to continue working in this manner.

Chapters 5, 6

Vocabulary: Across—4. lugubrious   5. feign   7. pretense   9. entourage   11. impassive   15. translucent   16. envision; Down—1. surreptitiously   2. tithe   3. connoisseur   6. invective   8. emissary   10. arduous   12. explicit

Questions: 1. Tree-ear's suspicions are aroused when Kang covers his work with a cloth as he wheels it to the kiln. He does this at a very early hour before anyone else will arrive, and he pushes his work to the farthest end of the kiln. This should ensure that it will protect special work from the curiosity of the other potters. 2. Tree-ear discovers that the bowls contain brick-red and white slip, which would not transform to celadon green when fired. He wonders what kind of success Kang has had with slip decoration because potters have been unsuccessful in the past. 3. As winter approaches, Tree-ear is worried that Crane-man will not have warm enough clothes, and he hates the cold nights in the dugout on the edge of the village to which they move in winter. 4. Crane-man acquires a warm winter jacket from Tree-ear who received it as a gift from Min's wife. She had made a quilted jacket and trousers for her son before he died and was happy to give them to Tree-ear as they had never been worn. Since the sleeves of the jacket were too long for Tree-ear, he gave it to Crane-man. 5. Kang has secretly developed a way to do inlay work on his pottery. Tree-ear doesn't reveal this secret to Min because he discovered the process by spying on Kang; he agrees with Crane-man who advises that taking Kang's idea by stealth would be stealing. 6. In response to the news of the emissary's visit, Min no longer sings at his wheel and works through his midday meal. His wife emerges from the house more often. And at the kiln, the potters no longer joke or smoke idly, but seem tense in anticipation. 7. Despite the inferior quality of his pottery, Tree-ear thinks Kang might receive a royal commission because his inlay technique is unique and striking, overshadowing the imperfections of his pottery. 8. Min thinks he might receive a commission after

Emissary Kim compliments his work and spends a long time looking over this pottery.

Chapters 7, 8

Vocabulary: 1. b 2. g 3. a 4. f 5. h 6. c 7. e 8. d; 1. plaintive 2. noxious 3. exulted 4. frenetically 5. remiss 6. haranguing 7. serenity 8. intricate

Questions: 1. Min sends Tree-ear for white and red clay because he wants to compete with Kang to create slip inlayed pottery before the emissary returns. 2. As Tree-ear drains the clay for Min, he realizes that he has acquired the skill of determining the proper consistency that clay must reach. He has gained this ability through practice, as Min has never given him direct instruction. 3. As he awaits the emissary's return, Min is more anxious, works with ferocity, and remains at the kiln for the entire period of the firing. He is alarmingly quiet instead of hurling orders at Tree-ear. This indicates that the commission is crucial to him. 4. Min smashes his own vases because he is angry that they all have brown spots caused by the firing, over which he has no control. 5. Tree-ear offers to journey to Songdo because the emissary believes Min will receive a royal commission if he can have an example of Min's inlay work, which he trusts will be better than that which provided Kang with a limited commission. Tree-ear feels that he will be repaying the kindness Min's wife offered him were he to travel in place of his aged master. 6. Min's wife will allow Tree-ear to travel if he promises to return quickly and safely and that he call her *Ajima*, or Auntie. This suggests that she is very fond of the boy. 7. Tree-ear fears the journey to Songdo because he has never before ventured beyond the village. He fears the unknown, the great distance, and the possibility of being attacked by robbers. Crane-man allays his fears by advising him to face his challenge one day at a time. 8. When Tree-ear asks Min to teach him how to make a pot, the potter angrily replies that he would only have passed on his skill to his son.

Chapters 9, 10

Vocabulary: 1. progressively 2. impeccable 3. grimacing 4. endeavor 5. trepidation 6. meager 7. decreed 8. foraging

Questions: 1. Tree-ear would not be able to find another master because it is a well-kept tradition throughout Korea that potters pass on their skills to their sons. 2. "A second door" refers to the opportunity that Tree-ear has to mold small pieces of clay by hand even if he is never taught to use the potter's wheel. 3. Ajima says she needs Crane-man's help and will provide meals for his services, and Tree-ear tells Crane-man that he does not want to have to worry about Ajima while he is away. Even though Crane-man recognizes Tree-ear's ploy, he accepts the offer because he realizes how important it is to him. 4. Crane-man is so moved by Tree-ear's gift that he is rendered speechless. When he can speak, he says he is honored to wear the monkey, which he attaches to his waist. 5. Min has shown Tree-ear so little affection in the past that even such a small gesture as a touch on the shoulder startles the boy. 6. Tree-ear's journey goes well: he enjoys the hospitality of country people, is able to find food and a place to stay every night, no mishap befalls him or his cargo, and the weather is fine. 7. Both Tree-ear and Crane-man are superstitious of foxes until they each face a fox, are not harmed, and subsequently lose their fear. 8. Crane-man wants Tree-ear to visit the rock of the Falling Flowers because that is the site where the women attending the King of Paekche leaped to their death, like falling flowers, rather than be taken by T'ang. Crane-man wants Tree-ear to see the site so that he will be inspired by the courage shown by the women. 9. It becomes urgent for Tree-ear to get Min's work work to Songdo when the boy notices that Kang's work has already been admired and replicated for sale on the streets of Puyo.

Chapters 11–13

Vocabulary: 1. i 2. c 3. f 4. a 5. j 6. b 7. h 8. d 9. e 10. g; 1. contorted 2. incredulous 3. welter 4. quell 5. radiance 6. pinioned 7. subdued 8. pallor 9. chastened 10. jovial

Questions: 1. The robbers are angry because they were looking for rice; they can't sell the vases, which are obviously gifts for the palace that nobody would dare buy. They break the vases out of anger and frustration. 2. Tree-ear decides not to leap from the cliff because he realizes that it will take more courage to face Min, he remembers his promise to Ajima, and he knows that Crane-man is waiting for him. 3. Tree-ear believes that the single shard might impress the emissary because it has part of an inlaid peony blossom with its stem and leaves, and its glaze is still clear and pure. 4. Emissary Kim is polite to Tree-ear, listens to him, and is willing to look at the shard; his assistant is dismissive of Tree-ear, calls him a brazen fool, and wants to throw him out of the palace. 5. When Emissary Kim awards Min a commission, the boy is happy beyond words. 6. When Tree-ear tells Min about the commission, the potter is quiet and solemn. Although happy about the commission, Min is sad because he must tell Tree-ear that Crane-man was killed when the bridge above him collapsed. 7. After Tree-ear's return, Min is gentler than he has ever been, and he even compliments his work on the little monkey. 8. Tree-ear is surprised when Min tells him to cut large logs to make a potter's wheel, one for the boy to use to help the potter fill the royal commission; Ajima surprises Tree-ear when she indicates that he is to live with her and Min. 9. Ajima gives Tree-ear a new name that shares a syllable with that of Min and Ajima's deceased son, indicating that they are adopting him. This not only signifies their affection for the boy, but it also means that Tree-ear will no longer be considered an outcast in his society.

NOTES: